My United States
Alabama

JO S. KITTINGER

Childre
An Imprint c

D1366468

For Andrea, a.k.a. Badger, who is discovering Alabama's wonders with me.

Content Consultant
James Wolfinger, PhD, Associate Dean and Professor
College of Education, DePaul University, Chicago, Illinois

Library of Congress Cataloging-in-Publication Data
Names: Kittinger, Jo S., author.Title: Alabama / by Jo S. Kittinger.
Description: New York, NY : Children's Press, an imprint of Scholastic Inc., [2018] | Series: A true book |
    Includes bibliographical references and index.
Identifiers: LCCN 2017025782 | ISBN 9780531231616 (library binding) | ISBN   9780531247129 (pbk.)
Subjects: LCSH: Alabama—Juvenile literature.
Classification: LCC F326.3 .K57 2018 | DDC 976.1—dc23
LC record available at https://lccn.loc.gov/2017025782

Photos ©: cover: Mark Reinstein/Getty Images; back cover ribbon: AliceLiddelle/Getty Images; back cover bottom: Justin Sullivan/Getty Images; 3 bottom: Joe Fox/age fotostock; 3 map: Jim McMahon; 4 left: Dave King/Getty Images; 4 right: Ambientideas/Dreamstime; 5 bottom: scisettialfio/iStockphoto; 5 top: Carol M. Highsmith/Buyenlarge/Getty Images; 7 top: Stephen Saks Photography/Alamy Images; 7 center top: Brian Lawdermilk/Getty Images; 7 center bottom: Carol M. Highsmith/Buyenlarge/Getty Images; 7 bottom: Underwood Archives/age fotostock; 8-9: Michael Hanson/Aurora Photos; 11: FotoNero/Shutterstock; 12: Kari Goodnough/Bloomberg/Getty Images; 13: I. Weber/age fotostock; 14: Joel Sartore/Getty Images; 15: kristianbell/Getty Images; 16-17: nashvilledino2/iStockphoto; 19: Jeffrey Greenberg/UIG/Getty Images; 20: Tigatelu/Dreamstime; 22 right: tkacchuk/iStockphoto; 22 left: Atlaspix/Shutterstock; 23 bottom right: UniversalImagesGroup/Getty Images; 23 top left: scisettialfio/iStockphoto; 23 center right: Ambientideas/Dreamstime; 23 top right: Garry Mitchell/AP Images; 23 center left: Dave King/Getty Images; 23 bottom left: anna1311/iStockphoto; 24-25: Carol M. Highsmith/Buyenlarge/Getty Images; 27: Ball playing among the Choctaw Indians (engraving), Dore, Gustave (1832-83) (after)/New York Public Library, USA/Bridgeman Art Library; 29: DEA PICTURE LIBRARY/age fotostock; 30 top left: DEA PICTURE LIBRARY/age fotostock; 30 top right: Atlaspix/Shutterstock; 30 bottom: Carol M. Highsmith/Buyenlarge/Getty Images; 31 bottom: Ed Vebell/Getty Images; 31 top: Harold Valentine/AP Images; 32: NG Images/Alamy Images; 33: World History Archive/Ann Ronan Collection/age fotostock; 34-35: Carol M. Highsmith/Buyenlarge/Getty Images; 36: Brynn Anderson/AP Images; 37: Allyson Praytor/Getty Images; 38: Bill Barksdale/Getty Images; 39: Carol M. Highsmith/Buyenlarge/Getty Images; 40 inset: Leslie Banks/Dreamstime; 40 bottom: PepitoPhotos/iStockphoto; 41: Erika Goldring/Getty Images; 42 top: JT Vintage/age fotostock; 42 center: Whitman Studio/Library of Congress; 42 bottom right: AP Images; 42 bottom left: Chip Somodevilla/Getty Images; 43 top left: AP Images; 43 center: Kevin C. Cox/Getty Images; 43 top right: Mark Elias/Bloomberg/Getty Images; 43 bottom left: Robert Alexander/Archive Photos/Getty Images; 43 bottom center: Jerry Coli/Dreamstime; 43 bottom right: Carrienelson1/Dreamstime; 44 top: Roxana Gonzalez/Dreamstime; 44 bottom right: tatui suwat/Shutterstock; 44 bottom left: SeanPavonePhoto/iStockphoto; 45 top left: fdastudillo/Getty Images; 45 top right: unknown1861/iStockphoto; 45 center: SAUL LOEB/AFP/Getty Images; 45 bottom: World History Archive/Ann Ronan Collection/age fotostock. Maps by Map Hero, Inc.

Scholastic Inc., 557 Broadway, New York, NY 10012

1 2 3 4 5 6 7 8 9 10 R 27 26 25 24 23 22 21 20 19 18

Front cover: USS *Alabama*

Back cover: A replica of the bus civil rights icon Rosa Parks rode on December 1, 1955

Welcome to Alabama

Find the Truth!

Everything you are about to read is true **except** for one of the sentences on this page.

Which one is **TRUE**?

T or F Alabama played a major role in the civil rights movement.

T or F Alabama fought on the side of the North during the Civil War.

Find the answers in this book.

Contents

THE BIG TRUTH!

Monarch
butterfly

What Represents Alabama?

Black bear

Mercedes assembly line

3 History

4 Culture

Camellia

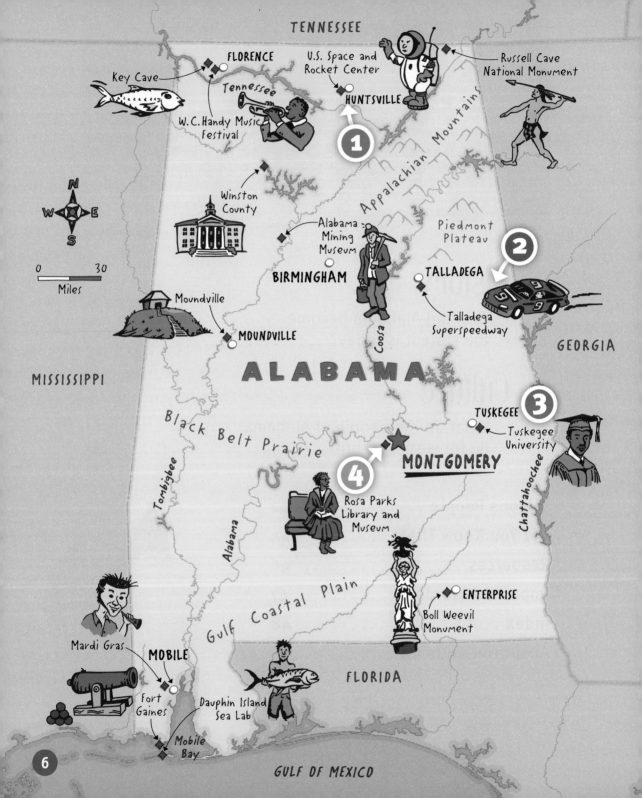

TENNESSEE

Key Cave

FLORENCE

U.S. Space and Rocket Center

Russell Cave National Monument

Tennessee

W. C. Handy Music Festival

HUNTSVILLE

①

Appalachian Mountains

N W E S

Winston County

Piedmont Plateau

Alabama Mining Museum

TALLADEGA

②

0   30
Miles

BIRMINGHAM

Talladega Superspeedway

GEORGIA

Moundville

MOUNDVILLE

Coosa

ALABAMA

TUSKEGEE

③

Tuskegee University

MISSISSIPPI

Black Belt Prairie

Tombigbee

MONTGOMERY

④

Chattahoochee

Alabama

Rosa Parks Library and Museum

Mardi Gras

MOBILE

Gulf Coastal Plain

ENTERPRISE

Boll Weevil Monument

Fort Gaines

Dauphin Island Sea Lab

FLORIDA

Mobile Bay

GULF OF MEXICO

This Is Alabama!

① U.S. Space and Rocket Center

In Huntsville, see a space shuttle, the *Saturn V* moon rocket, rocks from the moon, and more. Also tour the Marshall Space Flight Center.

② Talladega Superspeedway

This huge racetrack hosts some of the biggest races of the National Association for Stock Car Auto Racing (NASCAR). Visitors can check out the International Motorsports Hall of Fame and Museum and tour the track.

③ Tuskegee University

Tuskegee was founded in 1881 by African American educator Booker T. Washington to give former slaves a chance to get an education. Today, more than 3,000 students are enrolled.

④ Rosa Parks Library and Museum

This museum honors Rosa Parks, who helped launch the civil rights movement in 1955 when she refused to give up her seat on a bus to a white passenger.

When Lake Martin was created
in the 1920s, it was the largest
human-made lake in the world.

CHAPTER 1

Land and Wildlife

Alabama is a land of diverse and beautiful natural scenery. In the northeast, mountains and hills rise dramatically. Marshlands stretch along the state's southern border and white sand beaches cover its shoreline on the Gulf of Mexico. In between, you'll find rolling grasslands and forests. More than 4,000 caves have been discovered in Alabama, and several spectacular caverns are open for public tours.

The Lay of the Land

Alabama is in the southeastern United States. It is bordered by Tennessee to the north, Mississippi to the west, Georgia to the east, and Florida and the Gulf of Mexico to the south. Alabama is a medium-sized state both in landmass and population. Six major rivers flow through the state, and it has more than 1,350 miles (2,173 kilometers) of **navigable** water. That is more than any other state in the continental United States.

This map shows where the higher (orange and red) and lower (green) areas are in Alabama.

Cathedral Caverns

At Cathedral Caverns in northeastern Alabama, visitors can explore a cave system filled with **stalactites** and **stalagmites**. These incredible rock formations were created by water dripping through the limestone walls of the caves. The biggest stalagmite is called Goliath. It is a whopping 45 feet (14 meters) tall, 243 feet (74 m) around, and about 40 feet (12 m) thick. Cathedral Caverns became a state park in 2000.

Inside the caves, temperatures are comfortable year-round.

11

MAXIMUM TEMPERATURE 112°F

MINIMUM TEMPERATURE -27°F

Hurricane Katrina caused serious flooding and other damage in Alabama in 2005.

Climate

Winters are mild in Alabama, with only occasional snow in the north. Summers are hot and humid. Rain falls evenly year-round, but Alabama can get some dangerous storms. Tornadoes most often occur in March, April, and November. Every year, people are killed by these huge, swirling storms. Hurricanes are another threat. A serious hurricane makes a direct hit on the coast of Alabama about once every 16 years, causing major damage each time.

Plants

A rich variety of plant life can be found growing throughout Alabama's diverse landscape. Hardwood forests with oak, maple, and hickory trees provide shelter for ferns and wildflowers. Bald cypress trees and willows are found alongside tall, thick grasses in wetlands. Alabama is home to many rare wildflowers, including beautiful Cahaba lilies, which grow in swift-flowing water. **Carnivorous** pitcher plants trap insects and use them as a source of food.

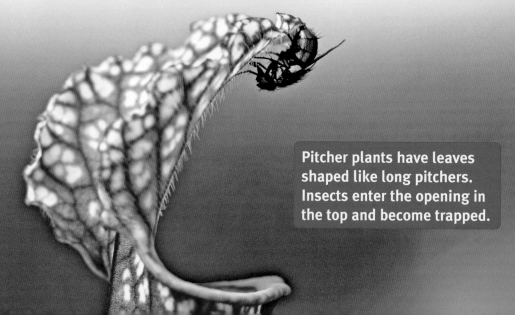

Pitcher plants have leaves shaped like long pitchers. Insects enter the opening in the top and become trapped.

Animals

Mammals commonly found in Alabama include squirrels, coyotes, and deer. At night, you are likely to see raccoons, armadillos, or skunks scurrying about. Around water, you might find otters, beavers, or muskrats. Black bears wander through parts of northern and southern Alabama, while bobcats roam the entire state. Wild hogs are known for destroying the state's crops and native plants. Alabama also has many species in danger of dying out, including the Alabama beach mouse.

Alabama beach mice burrow into sand dunes along the coast to create nests.

Six species of poisonous snakes live in Alabama, including the copperhead.

Alabama's rivers and lakes are home to more than 450 species of fish. This is more than any other state! Few states can top the number of bird species found in Alabama, either. They include majestic bald eagles, big brown pelicans, and tiny ruby-throated hummingbirds. The state's native reptiles include alligators, lizards, turtles, and many kinds of snakes. Rattlesnakes, copperheads, and water moccasins are poisonous snakes to watch out for.

CHAPTER 2

Government

Since becoming a state in 1819, Alabama has had three capitals. Cahaba, where the Cahaba and Alabama Rivers meet, was chosen as the first one. Cahaba often flooded, though, so Tuscaloosa was selected as the second capital in 1826. In 1846, state leaders decided to move the capital to a more central location—Montgomery. The capitol was constructed on "Goat Hill" in 1847, but it burned down two years later. It was rebuilt and has since been enlarged several times.

State Government Basics

Like other U.S. states, Alabama's government is divided into three branches. The legislative branch consists of the Senate and House of Representatives. They write new laws. The executive branch is headed by the governor. He or she carries out laws and creates the budget. The governor also approves or **vetoes** laws created by the legislative branch. The judicial branch is made up of the state's courts. It interprets and enforces the law.

ALABAMA'S STATE GOVERNMENT

LEGISLATIVE BRANCH
Writes and passes state laws

Senate (35 members)	House of Representatives (105 members)

EXECUTIVE BRANCH
Carries out state laws

Governor	Lt. Governor	Attorney General
Secretary of State	Commissioner of Agriculture and Industries	
Auditor	Treasurer	State Board of Education
Executive Budget Office	Public Service Commission	

JUDICIAL BRANCH
Enforces state laws

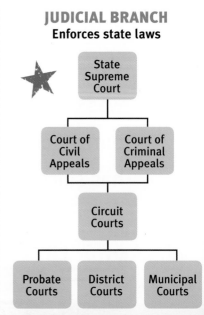

- State Supreme Court
  - Court of Civil Appeals
  - Court of Criminal Appeals
    - Circuit Courts
      - Probate Courts
      - District Courts
      - Municipal Courts

Bicycle police patrol the area around a ceramic tile mural of Alabama's state capitol

Our Right to Vote

Alabama's government officials make many decisions that affect the state's people. Citizens of all ages can participate in this process by writing or calling their state representatives to express their views. Elected officials pay attention to voters' thoughts. Citizens vote to elect their officials, and they can also vote them out of office in the next election. Voters can play an even greater role by getting involved in local government in their town or county.

Alabama's National Role

Each state elects officials to represent it in the U.S. Congress. Like every state, Alabama has two senators. The U.S. House of Representatives bases its numbers on a state's population. Alabama has seven representatives in the House.

Every four years, states vote on the next U.S. president. Each state is granted a number of electoral votes based on its number of members in Congress. With two senators and seven representatives, Alabama has nine electoral votes.

2 senators and 7 representatives

9 electoral votes

Alabama has a roughly average number of electoral votes.

Representing Alabama

Elected officials in Alabama represent a population with a range of interests, lifestyles, and backgrounds.

Ethnicity (2016 estimates)

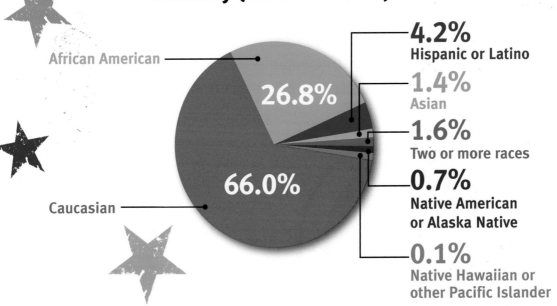

African American — 26.8%

Caucasian — 66.0%

4.2%
Hispanic or Latino

1.4%
Asian

1.6%
Two or more races

0.7%
Native American
or Alaska Native

0.1%
Native Hawaiian or
other Pacific Islander

3.5%
of Alabamians were
born in other countries.

68.7%
own their homes.

22.6%
are under the age of 18.

5.2%
of the state's citizens speak
a language other than
English at home.

48% male

52% female

84.3%
of the population
graduated from
high school.

23.5%
of the population
have a degree
beyond high school.

What Represents Alabama?

States choose specific animals, plants, and objects to represent the values and characteristics of the land and its people. Find out why these symbols were chosen to represent Alabama or discover surprising curiosities about them.

Seal

Alabama's state seal was designed in 1817, when the state was still a territory. It was created by William Wyatt Bibb, who was the territorial governor at the time. It shows all of the state's major rivers and bordering states. In 1868, Alabama changed its seal to an image of an eagle. However, it changed back to the original design in 1939.

Flag

Alabama's state flag was chosen in 1895. It was designed to resemble flags carried onto the battlefield by Alabama soldiers during the Civil War (1861–1865).

Alabama Red-Bellied Turtle

STATE REPTILE
This endangered turtle species is native to the waters of Alabama.

Camellia

STATE FLOWER
Native to Asia, these beautiful pink-and-red flowers were introduced to the American South.

Monarch Butterfly

STATE INSECT
This orange-and-black butterfly travels through Alabama each spring and fall.

Black Bear

STATE MAMMAL
This enormous animal roams Alabama's forests and can weigh up to 350 pounds (159 kilograms).

Peach

STATE TREE FRUIT
Alabama is home to many types of peaches, so it was no surprise when these sweet fruits were selected to represent the state.

Yellowhammer

STATE BIRD
Common throughout Alabama all year long, these woodpeckers are also known as northern flickers.

Prehistoric people built large mounds around the state. Visitors today can explore one site in Moundville.

Moundville Archaeological Park has exhibits showing the daily life of Alabama's early people.

CHAPTER 3

History

The earliest people in Alabama arrived more than 12,000 years ago. They hunted huge mammoths and mastodons. Giant ground sloths and armadillo-like creatures called glyptodonts roamed the land. Prehistoric graves, bone tools, jewelry, and pottery pieces have been found in Russell Cave in northern Alabama. These **artifacts** prove that people lived there for more than 10,000 years.

Native Americans

After the prehistoric people, many different Native American cultures arose in the state. The five major groups were the Alibamu, Chickasaw, Choctaw, Creek, and Coushatta. Cherokee also lived in the northeastern part of the state. Each of these cultures had their own beliefs and ways of living. Most Native Americans in Alabama planted corn, beans, and squash. They also hunted animals, caught fish, and collected plants for medicine and tea.

Alabama was named for a Native American group called the Alibamu.

This map shows some of the major tribes that lived in what is now Alabama before Europeans came.

Choctaws take part in a huge lacrosse game.

Alabama's Native American people built houses and towns. They told stories, created art, and played music. The Cherokee and Chickasaw peoples enjoyed a game called lacrosse. Huge teams would all play at once. At times, one group of people would fight another. But their way of life changed when Europeans arrived.

European Exploration

In 1540, Spanish explorer Hernando de Soto and his crew arrived in Alabama looking for gold. They killed and enslaved Native Americans as they traveled. French explorers landed in 1699. They built a settlement with a port on Massacre Island, off Alabama's coast. They were friendly toward the Native Americans. However, as more white people came to Alabama, battles with Native Americans increased. White men also brought diseases that killed many of the native peoples.

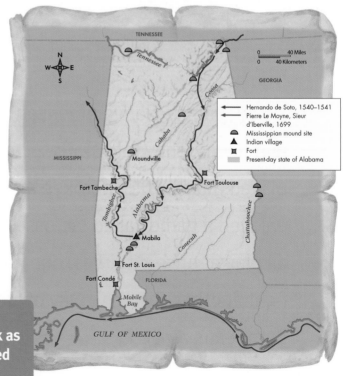

This map shows routes European explorers took as they explored and settled what is now Alabama.

Explorer Hernando de Soto explored much of what is now the southern United States.

Road to Statehood

The French worked from their port on Massacre Island to build a permanent settlement at Fort Louis, near what is now Mobile, in 1702. Over the following years, Spain and Great Britain also claimed parts of Alabama as their own. When the Revolutionary War (1775–1783) ended, so did British rule. Most of Alabama then became a U.S. territory. Spain later gave up its land claims. In 1819, Alabama became the 22nd state.

The Trail of Tears

In 1830, President Andrew Jackson signed the Indian Removal Act. Native Americans were forced to leave their homes in Alabama and other states. The U.S. government made the Cherokee march hundreds of miles to new Indian Territory in the West in 1838. Thousands died along the way. This journey became known as the Trail of Tears. Settlers poured into Alabama, taking the former Native American lands.

Timeline of Alabama Events

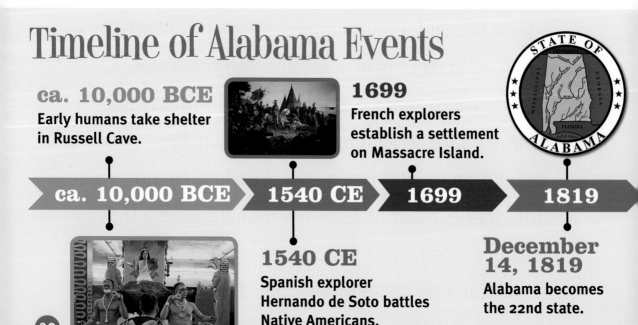

ca. 10,000 BCE
Early humans take shelter in Russell Cave.

1699
French explorers establish a settlement on Massacre Island.

| ca. 10,000 BCE | 1540 CE | 1699 | 1819 |

1540 CE
Spanish explorer Hernando de Soto battles Native Americans.

December 14, 1819
Alabama becomes the 22nd state.

Alabama in the Civil War

Just 42 years after becoming a state, Alabama **seceded** from the United States when the Civil War began. Cotton farming drove the state's economy. **Plantation** owners used slaves to work their fields. Alabama fought alongside other Southern states to preserve the practice of slavery. The North won the war in 1865, and Alabama's slaves were set free. Three years later, Alabama officially rejoined the United States.

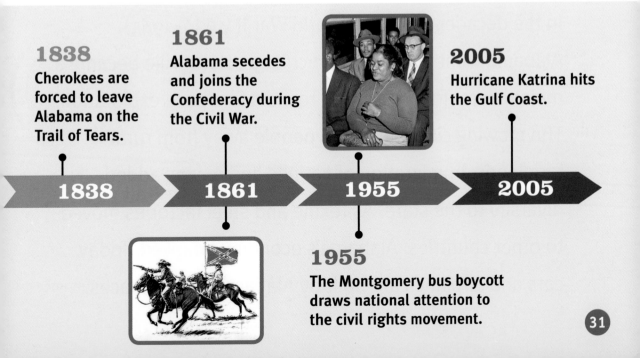

1838
Cherokees are forced to leave Alabama on the Trail of Tears.

1861
Alabama secedes and joins the Confederacy during the Civil War.

2005
Hurricane Katrina hits the Gulf Coast.

| 1838 | 1861 | 1955 | 2005 |

1955
The Montgomery bus boycott draws national attention to the civil rights movement.

Engineers and scientists at the Marshall Space Flight Center have worked to advance space exploration for more than 50 years.

Changing Times

In the decades following World War II (1939–1945), Alabama went through great change. Huntsville became a major center for developing rockets for space exploration. The growing cities attracted people away from rural farmlands. Immigration of Latinos and Asians added diversity to the state. As textile and steel factories moved to other countries, Alabama's economy **adapted**. Today, cars and airplanes are built by Alabamians of all races.

The "First Lady of Civil Rights"

Alabama was often in the middle of the civil rights movement of the 1950s and 1960s. Many important events in the movement took place in Birmingham, Selma, and Montgomery. In 1955, Rosa Parks refused to give up her seat on a bus to a white man. She was arrested, sparking the Montgomery bus **boycott**. Parks was later awarded the Congressional Gold Medal, the highest honor the United States can give a civilian.

The Montgomery Ballet performs a variety of ballet pieces.

CHAPTER 4

Culture

Alabama has a thriving arts culture. Concerts, museums, and plays are well attended. In Monroeville, local actors perform *To Kill a Mockingbird*, a story based on author Harper Lee's experiences growing up in the town. In Tuscumbia, *The Miracle Worker* is performed on the grounds of Helen Keller's home. The Alabama Shakespeare Festival is one of the largest in the world. Each year, children can audition to dance with the Alabama Ballet in *The Nutcracker*.

Alabama at Play

Football is king in Alabama. A huge rivalry exists between the University of Alabama and Auburn University teams. Alabamians enjoy other sports, too. Minor league baseball teams include the Birmingham Barons and Montgomery Biscuits. Golf is popular with locals and tourists. Fans flock to NASCAR races. Many Alabamians enjoy hunting and fishing. State parks offer camping, hiking, and boating. Alabama's beaches promise sun and fun.

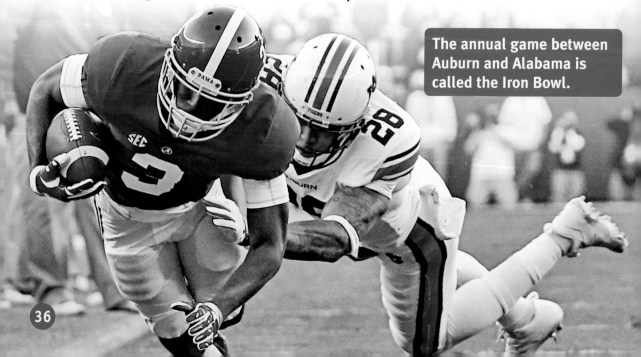

The annual game between Auburn and Alabama is called the Iron Bowl.

Some balloon pilots at the Alabama Jubilee offer rides to visitors.

Celebration, Alabama Style

Alabamians love to party! Festivals happen year-round. They celebrate music, art, and even peanuts! Mardi Gras, in Mobile, features dozens of parades. You can catch beads and Moon Pies as floats pass by. About 60 hot-air balloons fly during the Alabama Jubilee in Decatur. Birmingham's National Veterans Day Parade is one of the longest-running in the country. In December, check out the Galaxy of Lights in Huntsville. It's a miles-long display of lights!

A farmer holds a bunch of freshly harvested peanuts.

At Work

Alabama's economy was once driven almost entirely by farming. Today, much of the land is still used for **agriculture**. Important crops include cotton, pecans, peaches, and peanuts. In fact, about half the peanuts produced in the United States are grown within 100 miles (161 km) of Dothan! In cities, some people work in education, health care, aerospace, or steel production. Others build cars, airplanes, and other products.

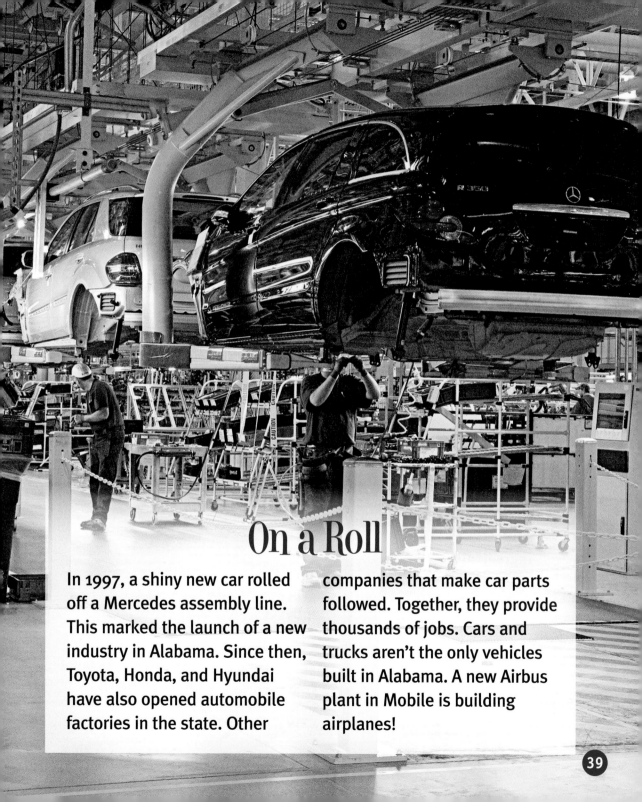

On a Roll

In 1997, a shiny new car rolled off a Mercedes assembly line. This marked the launch of a new industry in Alabama. Since then, Toyota, Honda, and Hyundai have also opened automobile factories in the state. Other companies that make car parts followed. Together, they provide thousands of jobs. Cars and trucks aren't the only vehicles built in Alabama. A new Airbus plant in Mobile is building airplanes!

Down-Home Cooking

Typical southern meals include foods such as fried chicken, black-eyed peas, turnip greens, and corn bread. An ice-cold glass of sweet tea will wash it all down. Order banana pudding for dessert! Alabama chefs often put a spin on traditional dishes like shrimp and grits. Locals love to cook out, grilling burgers and steaks. Alabama is also famous for delicious barbecue!

★ Barbecue Beef or Pork

Ask an adult to help you!

Contests are held in Alabama to see who cooks the best barbecue!

Ingredients

1 beef or pork roast, about 3 pounds
2 onions, chopped

½ cup water
1 medium-size bottle barbecue sauce
buns

Directions

Place the meat, onions, and water in a slow cooker. Cook on low for 6 to 8 hours. With an adult's help, shred the meat with a fork and return it to the pot. Pour the sauce over the meat, then heat everything for another 20 minutes or so on low. Serve the meat on buns.

Alabama is known for its southern hospitality and fierce loyalty to its football teams. The state trains astronauts and engineers. Musicians and authors find their voices here. People come from around the world for first-class medical treatment. There is richness to life in Alabama that comes from family, faith, and friendship. It is truly an amazing state! ★

Famous People

George Washington Carver

(ca. 1861–1943) was born a slave but achieved fame as a botanist, professor, and researcher. He developed hundreds of products using peanuts, sweet potatoes, and soybeans. He worked at Alabama's Tuskegee Institute for many years.

Harper Lee

(1926–2016) is the author of *To Kill a Mockingbird*. The book won a Pulitzer Prize and has been translated into more than 40 languages. She spent almost all of her life in Monroeville and based her famous novel on her hometown.

Helen Keller

(1880–1968) was the first deaf and blind person to earn a college degree. She went on to be an author, lecturer, and social activist. She was born in Tuscumbia.

Wernher von Braun

(1912–1977) was the director of NASA's Marshall Space Flight Center in Huntsville. His work helped send Americans to the moon.

Hank Aaron

(1934–) is considered one of the best baseball players of all time. He had a career total of 755 home runs. He was born in Mobile.

Condoleezza Rice

(1954–) is an author, professor, and political adviser. She served as national security adviser and then secretary of state under President George W. Bush. She was born in Birmingham.

Nick Saban

(1951–) is head coach of the University of Alabama football team. He led his team to five national championships and has received many Coach of the Year awards.

Octavia Spencer

(1970–) is an award-winning actress. She won an Academy Award for her role in *The Help* and was nominated for her role in *Hidden Figures*. She was born in Montgomery.

Davey Allison

(1961–1993) was a NASCAR driver who was inducted into the International Motorsports Hall of Fame in 1998. He lived in Birmingham.

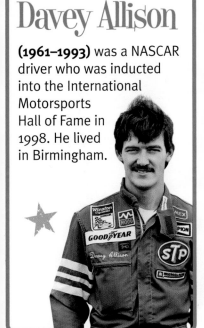

Bo Jackson

(1962–) is considered one of the greatest athletes of all time. He is the only person to be named an All-Star in both baseball and football! He was born in Bessemer.

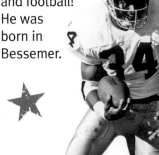

Did You Know That . . .

Growing cotton is an important part of Alabama's history and heritage.

The French named their first settlement Massacre Island because the beach was full of skeletons.

Alabama is the only state that has all the major natural resources needed to make iron and steel.

Russell Cave in Bridgeport is the site of Alabama's earliest known human inhabitants.

Dothan, Alabama, is the "Peanut Capital of the World." The world's largest peanut festival is held there each fall.

In 2017, President Barack Obama signed a proclamation creating the Birmingham Civil Rights National Monument, a site honoring Birmingham's major role in the civil rights movement.

Did you find the truth?

T Alabama played a major role in the civil rights movement.

F Alabama fought on the side of the North during the Civil War.

Resources

Books

Nonfiction

Hamilton, John. *Alabama: The Yellowhammer State*. Minneapolis: ABDO, 2017.

Kallio, Jamie. *What's Great About Alabama?* Minneapolis: Lerner Publications Company, 2015.

Somervill, Barbara A. *Alabama*. New York: Children's Press, 2014.

Fiction

Lee, Harper. *Go Set a Watchman*. New York: Harper, 2015.

Lee, Harper. *To Kill a Mockingbird*. Philadelphia: Lippincott, 1960.

Wilson, E.O. *Anthill: A Novel*. New York: W.W. Norton & Co., 2010.

Visit this Scholastic website for more information on Alabama:
★ www.factsfornow.scholastic.com
Enter the keyword **Alabama**

Important Words

adapted (uh-DAPT-id) changed because you are in a different situation

agriculture (AG-rih-kuhl-chur) the raising of crops and animals

artifacts (AHR-tuh-faktz) objects made or changed by human beings, especially tools or weapons used in the past

boycott (BOI-kaht) the refusal to buy something or do business with someone as a punishment or protest

carnivorous (kahr-NIV-ur-uhs) having meat as a regular part of the diet

navigable (NAV-ih-guh-buhl) deep enough and wide enough to allow the passage of ships

plantation (plan-TAY-shuhn) a large farm that produces crops such as cotton, coffee, sugar, and tea

seceded (sih-SEED-ed) to have formally withdrawn from a group or an organization, often to form another organization

stalactites (stuh-LAK-tites) icicle-shaped mineral deposits that hang from the roofs of caves

stalagmites (stuh-LAG-mites) mineral deposits that stick up from the floors of caves

vetoes (VEE-tohz) stops a bill from becoming law

Index

Page numbers in **bold** indicate illustrations.

About the Author

Jo S. Kittinger moved to Alabama when she was 12 and has lived in the Birmingham area ever since. She loves Alabama's diversity, with wooded mountains, sugar-white beaches, and forests full of wildlife. You might find her kayaking on Alabama's beautiful rivers! Jo is the author of more than 25 books for children.

NOV 16 2018